ISBN 978-0-259-48872-9
PIBN 10028897

1 MONTH OF
FREE
READING

at
www.ForgottenBooks.com

By purchasing this book you are eligible for one month membership to ForgottenBooks.com, giving you unlimited access to our entire collection of over 1,000,000 titles via our web site and mobile apps.

To claim your free month visit: www.forgottenbooks.com/free28897

English
Français
Deutsche
Italiano
Español
Português

www.forgottenbooks.com

Mythology Photography **Fiction**
Fishing Christianity **Art** Cooking
Essays Buddhism Freemasonry
Medicine **Biology** Music **Ancient
Egypt** Evolution Carpentry Physics
Dance Geology **Mathematics** Fitness
Shakespeare **Folklore** Yoga Marketing
Confidence Immortality Biographies
Poetry **Psychology** Witchcraft
Electronics Chemistry History **Law**
Accounting **Philosophy** Anthropology
Alchemy Drama Quantum Mechanics
Atheism Sexual Health **Ancient History**
Entrepreneurship Languages Sport
Paleontology Needlework Islam
Metaphysics Investment Archaeology
Parenting Statistics Criminology
Motivational

HALF HOURS WITH AN OLD GOLFER

BY

"CALAMO CURRENTE"

ILLUSTRATED BY

G. A. LAUNDY

LONDON

GEORGE BELL AND SONS

1895

R 23

CHISWICK PRESS:—CHARLES WHITTINGHAM AND CO.
TOOKS COURT, CHANCERY LANE, LONDON.

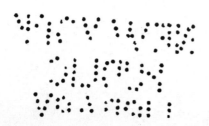

CONTENTS.

LIST OF ILLUSTRATIONS.

COLOURED PLATES.

ILLUSTRATIONS IN THE TEXT.

GOLF.

THE MAN WHO MISSED THE BALL.

GOLF.

1894.

" The man for wisdom's various arts renown'd,
Long exercised in woes, O Muse ! resound."

HOMER. (Pope.)

HE man who makes our lawns and links
abound
With clubs and balls, O Heavenly
Muse ! resound.
The man who when his arms have
wrought the fall
Of driver supple, fails to hit the ball—
The man who slices and is doomed to stray
From place to place in fields of promised hay—
The stormy turmoil of the human mind
In him who seeks a ball he cannot find—
The bunkered hazard and all other woes
The varied troubles of the game disclose—
Those thrills ecstatic from the pure delight

Of straight and true and distance judged aright—
The bracing muscles nerved to dire decision—
The passing fear of failure and derision,
In mercy sing—the outline of the shins
Of great attempted skill that seldom wins;
And spare! O spare the wonders that evolve
In postures quaint from clubs as they revolve
Around devoted heads of bravest men
Who try the game and fail, but try again;
Proclaim the virtues of the graceful fair
Who now for golf and all its joys declare,
Those artless gestures that announce success,
The tiny squeal of beauty in distress
(Unfailing attributes of loveliness);
.Relate the prowess of the southern host
That half a thousand golf-links now can boast
In merry England, till each echo rings,
Nor cease thy praises of the game for kings—
A game that brings dyspeptic man by stealth
To cull the pleasures that improve the health—
Which offers all that's muscular and mild
To charm the aged or allure the child,
T' enthrall our manhood, captivate the boy,
And yield the love of freedom we enjoy.

"GREAT ATTEMPTED SKILL."

Nor fail to picture to th' aspirant's mind
The Olympic attitudes he tries to find :
And guide his reason and his hand alike,
When with his driver he attempts to strike—
His feet, his hands, his back, his knees, and toes
In symmetry of force and graceful pose
Do thou arrange to Nature's own delight,
For Nature shuns the wrong and loves the right—
From out the latent principles of force
Bestow on man some precepts for the course,
That all may profit, though not all excel
   In geometric skill, in poise and stroke,
And that, applied to brains and thews as well,
   May rouse to rapture, or our wit provoke.

And Thou, mysterious grace of Love Divine,
   Be ever present to enoble all,
To curb the temper, lead us to incline
   To upright actions, if we act at all ;
Expel the false developments of pride
   That often lead intelligence astray,
That chase all virtue, that is prone to hide
   When faulty motives, human actions, sway !

JOHNNY CAMERON'S ORIGIN OF THE GAME.

"THEY CITE OOR AUNCIENT DADDIE."

JOHNNY CAMERON'S ORIGIN
OF THE GAME.

IT is nae jist exauckly kent
    Whaure gowfin first began ;
  A guid wheen gowfers have declared
    It's natr'l unto man.
    Tha pruifs they gie are something keen
  They cite oor auncient daddie,
An' say he lived upon the green,
  But never was a cadet ;
At least we a' may weel admit
  That Adam's often quoted,
An like a' unnerstannin' men
  For putters he was noted.

Then Cain he liked a heavy club
  To lay his brither deed ;

Methusalah had mony ties,
    His match he never dreed.
And syne guid Noah frae the Ark
    Sent oot a bonny skimmer,
An later on an awfu' lie
    Laid deed a man an's limmer.

Tha Greeks were sair in want o' gowf
    Whan Styx wus lost in Pandy,
An' to recover them the task
    Wus gi'en to worthy Sandy.
Since syne thro' mony ups and doons
    Auld Sandy's sons have made it,
Noo gowf is ca'd the wale o' games
    By them that's often played it.

Then here's a health to clubs an' baas
    To hoary men an' laddies
That mak the play as it shid be,
    But hang dishonest caddies.

AN ENGLISHMAN'S OPINION OF GOLF, IN 1870.

AN ENGLISHMAN'S OPINION OF GOLF, IN 1870.

WHERE limpid rills
Forsake the hills
And dream their way to sea—
Where gorse and sand
And grassy land
Make up the varied lea—
'Tis there a game
Unknown to fame,
Though played by many a Scot,
For ages past
Its charm has cast
Around the favoured spot.

All o'er the Links
The putting rinks
Are centred by a hole

In which, denotes,
A flag that floats,
The number of the goal.
The flags are few
And lead the view
Among the mazy gorse,
Eighteen—no more—
Are dotted o'er
Some Scottish miles, of course.

With careful aim,
To play the game,
A man must persevere
With such a will
To master skill,
And patience so sincere,
It seems to me
We'll never see
The merry south allured
To stand the fall
That club and ball
For temper have secured.

A German's Idea of Golf

A TEUTONIC IDEA OF GOLF.

DER Pritisher ee liksh die shport
    Ash Deutschers liksh die Laager,
Und ovendendimes ich lieb der zort
    Off came dat's comink swagger.
      Der Colf ist shoost die pesht, I dinks,
Off doshe mien hant I'fe dried in,
Vor id vill stronk make on die Links
      Philosophie,
      Psychologie,
Und all man hash zome bride in.

Do blay dish came you dakes some prains
    Und dink ash hard ash gan pe,
Die muskles musht doo dake mush bains,
    Der'sh nodink mampee-banpee ;
Ash iv indo die ewigkeit

Zome palls co lofly shkeemink,
  Und den you valk
  Und laugh und talk
Ash vree ash poet's dreamink.

À LA FRANÇAISE.

ONSIEUR L'ANGLAIS, wat you go
    To do wis all zie stiks?
You strike zie ball—you walk sometime,
    And zen you's in zie fix;
You dig zie sand—you plough zie field,
You go zrough all zie wet,
You look so anxious, work so hard,
Your brow would almost sweat.
And zis you call a sportingk game
    In bottes de l'Engleterre!
O Monsieur, you fatigue yourself!
    Your mind and muskles spare!

"O MONSIEUR, YOU FATIGUE YOURSELF!"

TWA SCOTCH CADDIES IN LONDON.

"GET OOT MY SIGHT, YOU MUCKLE BRUTE."

TWA SCOTCH CADDIES IN LONDON.

[SANDY: heard of a good birth for a professional at the —— Club.

JOHN: came to London to look out for such a place, but had not heard of one. They travelled together, and, becoming still closer friends, they took a room near Euston. Sandy wrote at once to the Hon. Treasurer of the —— Club, who called to arrange with him. Subsequently the following conversation, or something to the same effect, took place.]

"AN Jock, I never thought that gowf
    Wad tak a had sae freely
Among they bletherin' English folk
    Wi' mouth that's aye sae mealy.
The siller scatters awfu' free,
  The glesses aye are clinkin',
Ods, Jock, I'm no gaun bak tae North
  An that's what I've been thinkin'."

"Aweel! Aweel!" then John replies,
　"If that's yer set decision
You'll find a usefu' friend in me,
　For I've got full provision :
Twa pound a week, a house and fire,
　An' garden grund in plenty,
The links a' under my control
　Are jist a wee thing benty ;
I'm just gaun hame to wed my lass,
　An' syne I tak possession,
Although I was a caddie yince,
　I'm noo in the profession."

"I'm gled o' that, man Jock my frien',
　We'll hae a canty time o't
For I've come here to find a place
　That suits me to the rhyme o't ;
I missed the gentleman the day,
　He'd jist come here an' lost me—
'Twas for the place that I cam south,
　No carin' what it cost me."

Then Sandy's friend "Ye neednae gang,
　You're sure to be rejected,

For I cam up wi' letters three,
   The Treasurer's respected.
He axed for you, I maun confess,
   But that was your affair, man,
We had a blether ower a gless,
   An clean I nicked him there, man.

" I had a letter frae oor laird
   That fairly made me winner,
The laird's the Treasurer's uncle's son
   As I'm a living sinner:—
But Sandy, man, your frien' I'll be,
   I need a man to stay me,
I'll staun ye fifteen bob a week,
   Though that'll hardly pay me."

" Get oot my sight, you muckle brute
   Is now the light rejoinder,
To which complacently says John,
   " I thought ye'd ta'en it kinder,
It's after a' the rin' o' luck
   A stimie has been laid ye,
You've lost your temper i' the game,
   But I'se no daur upbraid ye ! '

HOW TO LEARN THE GAME.

"FORE!"

HOW TO LEARN THE GAME.

A MAN of character, in whatever he undertakes, will always show some individuality in his *modus operandi.* It is individuality that gives the final touches to a picture, the finish to a statue, or the phrasing to a musical composition. Nothing human being perfect it becomes clear that in aiming at the golden garment, we must not expect to get more thereof than the hem : in science the hem is narrow, in art it is a little broader. To my mind art is flimsy if it do not include its relative science. The painter or sculptor who does not trouble himself, at least in the beginning, with fundamental principles such as prismatic colours, form, analysis of the beautiful, etc., does not deserve to succeed.

The man who knows nothing of acoustics and the laws of the beautiful in motion may be a very good fiddler, but he should not call himself a musician. To be level with the musical possibilities of our time, a composer or (in a less degree) a performer should not only be at home in his own particular science and art, but he should be on intimate visiting terms with all subjects however distantly related. Unfortunately, this is so seldom the case that music has gone backwards instead of forwards for the last twenty-five years.

While art has been standing still, Invention has, hand in hand with mechanics, gone at a terrific speed. The science of education has been jostled about by destructive instruction. And man is now, as he always was, more or less the creature of circumstances. The professional golfer, the teacher of music, the schoolmaster and many other individuals, as a rule, seem to have neglected to study the anatomy of their respective subjects.

Instead of offering instructions entirely founded upon individuality, the writer will here endeavour to suggest such methods as may educate the beginner according to his individual nature, which will be this, that or the other, according to former education and habit. Many of the hints will be at variance with the experience of first-class players, but in the writer's opinion the first-class player often fails in the art of concealing art. The writer imagines—perhaps vainly imagines—that he can prove the correctness of such of his instructions as are at variance with prevalent methods, but at the worst even those gentlemen who have written so charmingly upon the subject, will allow that an aspirant will do well to go through the writer's discipline as a preparation for their elaborate instructions.

HOW TO LEARN THE GAME.

THE DRIVER—LENGTH AND MAKE.

IF you stand quite erect, with your club
at your toe,
Then the shaft of your driver should
be
Just the length that will reach to your
elbow, or so—
Neither longer nor shorter for me ![1]
If the handle be supple the chances are great
That you won't sprain your wrist, it is true,
But unless you are certain of driving quite straight
A good stiff one's the handle for you :
As a matter of course
The stiff club requires force
And it wont drive so far at the best,
But no fact is made plainer
Than, that he is the gainer
Who can judge whereabout he will rest.

[1] Home practice is best to begin golf.

D

As to weight, it is clearly according to strength,
So we can't have a rule like to that for the length.

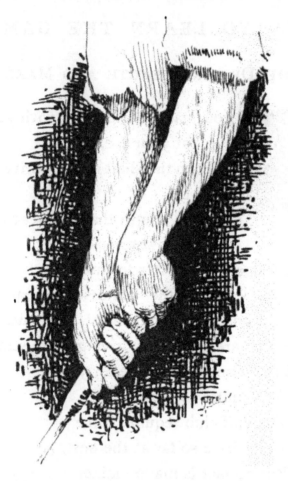

How to hold it—The Grip.

The best of players do not trouble much,
Instinctive guidance regulates their touch ;

But this is certain, that the grip should be
The left hand tightly, and the right more free,
For thus the left may regulate the line
While right and left, to make the stroke, combine ;
The largest knuckles of the thumbs should stand
Above the handle somewhat ; and the hand
Should grasp the shaft with firm, unerring grip—
Not fast and loose—or else the fingers slip.

How to Use It.

THE hands well practised and the grip attained,
We now may think of how the swing is gained :
Not only noting all that must be done,
But marking well the errors we must shun.[1]
In passing, let us clearly understand
We seek to help the inexperienced hand :
Intended errors here and there secure
Our ends, as poison doth a frequent cure.
The earliest fault that's likely to arrive
Is, with imperfect grip, to have a drive.
Be warned in time—make perfect—nothing less

[1] The hands should be close together.

"THIS POSE ESTABLISHED WITH THE GRIP COMBINED."

Each short instruction, to attain success.
The grip now perfect, hold the club that so
The elbows, knuckles, and the club below
Are nearly lined : then on the level ground
Two thirds your club-length parted shall be found,[1]
Your feet, in square position, heels and toes
All resting firmly as in measured rows ;
Then next observe the ankle and the knee
Must bend to yield more elasticity.
This pose established with the grip combined,
You then must drill the wrists, their ease to find.
The body, arms and legs the pose retain
While wrists alone the exercise maintain
Until with ease, and in one inclined plane,
The club shall swing and skim the ground again.
This drill continue till 'tis clearly seen
You've gauged the level and just touch the green.[2]

Our next adventure now the swing shall be,
In which 'tis hard to attain dexterity.
Now hold the club as you have done before,
The sole upon the ground it passes o'er,

[1] Outside measurement.
[2] If all positions be tested before a mirror success will be doubly secured.

"YOU THEN MUST DRILL THE WRISTS, THEIR EASE TO FIND."

Then try what travel you can give the head,
Not moving arms nor wrists but in their stead,
The shoulders, knees, and ankles :—by degrees
A semicircle you describe with ease.
But mark this well, the perfect feat attain
By motion ever in one constant plane ;
The club face always at right angles to it—
Don't learn to twist the club, or you will rue it;
The eye must never wander from the spot
Where you would have the ball to play a shot.
The club should touch the ground at every swing,
To gauge the level true is everything.

So far the feet have never left the ground :
You now must try again till you have found
That as the club to left or right ascends
A rising heel some useful inches lends ;
'Tis natural that when we swing to right
The left heel in the end, its greatest height
Attains ! and *vice versâ*, until art
Full harmony to motion shall impart—
No nervous twitch—but give and take—shall so
Compel the club to yield a perfect blow.

"SLOW TO THE RIGHT YOU SWING."

Then most important in each future case—
(Like rallentando when performed with grace)—

"AN IDEAL FINISH."

Slow to the right you swing, whilst on the fall
Accelerando as you near the ball :
But ere this point is reached it will be found

The right heel rises, and the left doth bear
Th' increasing weight, thrown forward in a bound
To drive a long one, if the feat we dare.
Meanwhile remember at a point between
The right and left, both heels are on the green ;
If on both feet by accident you rise
At once you spoil th' attempted enterprise.
Again, the toe should never leave the spot
To it assigned : and, whether raised or not,
The ankle must not twist but bend with grace,
That so again the heel may find its place.
All this achieved by careful exercise
A combination is a glad surprise ;
But let no childish haste our progress stay,
Complete the swing before you try to play !

When on reluctant wrists we did our will
And forced them into unaccustomed drill
The grip was central to describe an arc,
So in the later swing you may remark
'T was still an arc but with a radius found
Between some point within us and the ground—
One point between the glenoids we suppose,
The other where th' imagined ball arose.

Now with the arms alone—the wrists denied,
The head and body still—from side to side
Once more essay a slow and easy swing
As far to right as you, the club, can bring,
And nearly in that plane you now must know—
Not waving—curling—twisting as you go.
When, three times running, you can skim the ground
Your drill is finished—soon the swing is found.
In future we must know as 1, 2, 3,
These arc-like swings, to avoid verbosity.

The perfect swing comprises all we've done,
The grip and 1, 2, 3, combined in one ;
The arcs with moving centres thus produced
To no true circle now may be reduced,
Except by few whose supple joints permit
The right-hand swing to meet the point we hit.
But as we aim at normal ease and grace,
The circle by a scroll we must replace ;
Yet bear in mind, the nearer you can bring
The scroll into the circle in the swing,
The better you will drive—the more confess
That golf is just a game of loveliness.

One final exercise without the ball,
Which conquered, you will have success in all.

As if about to drive, now take your place,
Address th' imagined ball with ease and grace,
Try 1, 2, 3, in such a way that each
The same proportions of its scope shall reach.[1]

Forgive reiteration—slowly back—
   The gaze unerring, ever must remain
Upon th' imagined ball, the guarded track
   Of club head must not wander from the plane.

Whenever thrice consecutively, thus,
   Fulfilling all conditions you shall hit
Th' attempted ball with moderate impetus,
   Then on the welcome globe we try your wit.

To screen all imperfections from the ken
Of grinning caddies and satiric men,
Procure at once " The Game of Golf " at home,
At which you may resolve all doubts that come,
For every ball comes meekly rolling back,
Your club inviting to another whack.

[1] *i.e.* 1, 2, 3, begin together and move in unison till all three
finish together.

In 1, you may remember, how the play
We gave the wrists compelled the arms to sway
The club, in easy curves, not stiff and straight,
With elbows out for space to compensate ;
By No. 1 you therefore measure best
Where you should stand, and where the ball should
       rest.
You we now leave, to half a gross of strokes
     Without a tee—the ball on level ground—
At first this practise any man provokes,
     'T will tell hereafter when you play the round.

A RULE FOR THE POSITION.

THE destined direction, whatever the pose,
Is the line you should touch with the points of your
          toes ;
The pose will depend on the drive you would make,
If its high, the ball's forward ; low, more in the wake.
Then the left foot should always be nearer the hole
     Than the club when the ball you address ;
If you get the ball foremost you'll loose the control,
     And have many sad things to confess.

IN the diagram A B is the line of direction, E is the left and F is the right. Both feet touch this line in making a full drive, C D is also a line of direction on

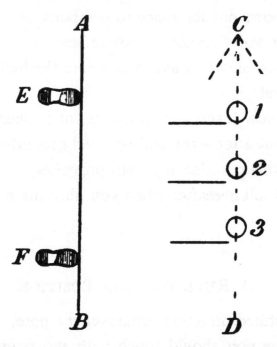

which the ball should be found somewhere between the positions 1 and 3. If the ball be at 1 it should make a long carry without a run. At 2 it should carry well and run also. At 3 the club strikes the ground and is arrested, while the ball, if hit, shoots off without much rise, excepting at the tail of the stroke. It used to be frequently made with the " Baffin spuin " out of a cuppy lie. Of course these effects can only be produced by a clean hit ball, the arms following on except in the last instance, when the ground must not be hard, and the club should not be forced by strength of grip and arm.

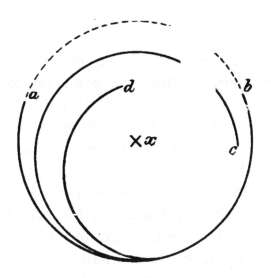

x = centre.

a b is a good short swing.

c b is a good long swing.

d b is bad. The nearer *c b* comes to the complete circle, as suggested, the better the swing.

N.B. Taking the driver as measured, as a standard for proportionate clubs, we may readily ascertain their proper sizes by reference to the following table. (They must be measured in the same vertical position as the driver.) If we represent the driver by the number 44, the respective proportions of the other clubs would be :—

Brassey = 44.
Cleek, Iron and Brassey Niblick = 41.
Mashie = 40.
Niblick = 39.
Putter = 37.

If we depart from these proportions the result will be :—with shorter clubs we shall be compelled to stoop too much or to play the ball too near us ; while with longer clubs we shall neither be able to bend sufficiently, nor to play with the ball at the proper distance. The shorter clubs would be too upright, the longer ones too flat. Choose your clubs of similar pitch. If properly pitched the toe and heel of the club should touch the level ground when you hold it in position for addressing the ball.

It is true that long men have played well with short clubs and short men with long ones ; and even such an accomplished authority as Mr. Hutchinson leaves the tyro to his fancy. It seems to me, however, that while the long man errs on the safe side in using short clubs ; the short man, who uses a long club, not only exposes himself to ridicule, but is sure to lose in other respects what he may gain in speed. It must be borne in mind that the writer does not pretend to say that every player should restrict himself to the use of clubs of the prescribed length. What is meant is practically :—if you are a beginner and wish to learn to play a respectable game in the shortest

ON THE GREEN.

G.A.L

possible time, you must carry everything into practice methodically ; and your clubs must be of the most convenient weight and dimensions. The proportions given are a little inclined to be under rather than over the exact sizes, and for this reason, that the shorter the handle to a tool the easier is it used. The only difference in using longer clubs would be a few feet in the stroke, which in nine cases out of ten would be more than counterbalanced by foozles.

Various strokes necessary for first-class play.

FULL DRIVE.

IF 1, 2, 3 are perfect now,
    Combined as when apart,
A careful study of the strokes
    With practice gains the art.

The combination 1, 2, 3,
    To all the clubs applies :
We use the clubs according to
    The nature of the lies.

If clear on even grass we find
    Our ball inviting lies,
We take the driver, when the stroke
    The distant flag implies.

E

But if, in such a case, the lie
   Suggest the smallest doubt,
The Brassie is the club to use
   To bring you safely out.

If still more doubtful, take the cleek ;
   If bad, the iron play ;
If very bad, the mashie's best
   To get the ball away.

If lieing in a mossy groove,
   The niblick brass may serve ;
For hidden cup or in the sand
   The niblick we reserve.

Full drives you now may understand
   With any tool, is made,
Except the putter, which alone
   Upon the green is played.

TABLE OF FAIRLY GOOD FULL DRIVES OFF THE
VARIOUS CLUBS.

Driver	160 yards
Brassie.	150 „
Cleek	140 „
Iron.	120 „
Mashie.	100 „
Brassie niblick	130 „

WE now fully understand that all the clubs except
the putter
May be used in combination 1, 2, 3.
But the driver or the brassie, or the brassie niblick,
never
Should be used unless the drive be full and free.

But the cleek, the iron, and mashie, in a multitude of
cases
May be used in half a dozen varied ways
To produce effects in distance—lofting, cutting, jerk-
ing, shooting,
By the golfer who, a perfect style, essays.

But although you may consider this is very compli-
  cated,
 You will find that you can trace it to the drive,
If you only practise fairly all the exercise suggested,
 From which all other motions we derive.

There are differences truly in the balance and positions,
 And the difficulty naturally found
In becoming quite familiar with their use and appli-
  cation,
 On the links, when we attempt to play a round.

These various strokes, in order of relation
 To what you must have practised, we shall take,
Without regard to fine manipulation
 Of cuts or other niceties of brake.

↑
.ɔc

e	5	6	f		o	15	16	p
d	4	7	g		n	14	17	q
c	3	8	h		m	13	18	r
b	2	9	i		l	12	19	s
a	1	10	j		k	11	20	t

Diagram of all possible reasonable positions.
Scale, 1 *inch to the foot.*

In referring to the above diagram, the following abbreviations may be used :—

ɔc = the line of direction. R = the right foot. L = the left foot. h = the heel. t = the toe. B = the ball.

By means of this diagram, which is merely a development upon the first position for the drive, we shall readily acquire the varied appropriate positions for approach strokes, etc.

Full Drive.

R has t in 1 and h in a.

L „ t „ 5 „ h „ e.

High drive, B in p.

Low „ B „ q.

Shooter drive, B in r.

Action = equals 1, 2, 3 (as before explained) in combination.

Grip—left, tight ; right, loose.

This applies to the driver- or brassie-play. The same applies to all full drives excepting that :—

With the cleek, iron, mashie, or brassie-niblick, you have for

> High drive, B in 16.
> Low „ B „ 17.
> Shooter drive, B in 18.

With the niblick, B is in 15, 14, or 13, according to circumstances.

Three-Quarter Stroke.

(Cleek, iron, or mashie.)

Stand as for full drive.

Keep shoulders and body still.

Do not raise the heels.

Grip with both hands.

THREE-QUARTER STROKE.

Otherwise, as for full drive, allowing the arms to follow on, in the line of direction.

N.B.—B is at 17. Possible result as implied, *i.e.*, three-quarters of the distance of full drive. .

HALF STROKE.

(Different position.)

R has t in i and h in 10.

L „ t „ 5 „ h „ d.

B in 18 or 19.

(N.B. This scale is suitable to a man of 5 ft. 10½ in. The respective positions will always be the same, but the measurements will vary. As the scale is one inch to the foot, we may measure if we vary the scale in exact ratio to the height. It must also be borne in mind that the proportions are those of an athlete. Allowance must be made for any variation in the man : even thus the positions will be right.)

Action as in exercise 1, with slight use of right forearm.

Do not grip so rigidly with the left : but, hold well with the thumb and first finger of the right.

The shorter the stroke, the more weight should be borne by the right leg.

Knees conveniently bent.

Left arm firm.

HALF STROKE.

Left wrist and hand must return to the exact place they occupied on addressing the ball.

Arms do not follow.

Probable result, as implied.

WRIST STROKE.

Much the same position as for the Half Stroke, but the right elbow is bent and away from the body. Left remains almost stationary to serve as a hinge-centre for the movement of the club.

Grip—Not too tight anywhere.

Fingers do the nice work. Thumb and first of right hand do not loosen.

This stroke is often assisted by a movement of the knees, which, in the writer's opinion, is neither useful nor graceful. It is like putting out one's tongue to help one to write. Of course it helps the distance, but the wrists can do that if they be trained properly.

Under favourable circumstances, these strokes may be varied by placing B in 19 or 20, and by slicing B, across the line of direction, with the club kept at right angles to it.

The position is, face the hole and stand so as to admit free action for a twisted club. This stroke is generally a work of supererogation.

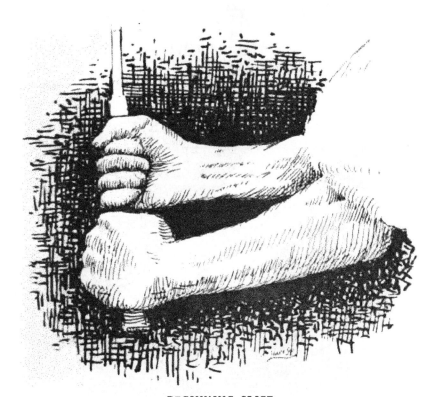

BEGINNING SLICE.

FINISH OF THE QUARTER STROKE.

It probably had its origin in the fact that Scotch laddies play with limited tools, and cut with the cleek when they don't possess an iron. As this produces a right diagonal spin, it checks the roll and turns the ball to the right of the loft.

There are times when the cross cut is of great advantage, just as one may slice a full drive around an obstacle. Many prefer under cut, or a high loft. It is difficult to gauge, but it is charming.

(N.B.—A pier-glass or a snap-shot camera might be of great use for the criticism of your own movements.)

PUTTING.

You are recommended to try to get your putter to work like a pendulum, with the wrists for a hinge. The position is about the same as for the wrist stroke.

Do not get into the absurd habit of taking a very short hold. If you fancy your club isn't balanced, take a little of the weight away. If you are clever at tricks of motion, and have very steady as well as supple hands and wrists, you need never lean the arm upon the body to steady your putting. If it be otherwise, lean the arm where you find it helps you. When you know how to put and play generally, cultivate the art of concealing art.

Supposing that you have got up these lessons faithfully, I will now revert to doggerel, and invite

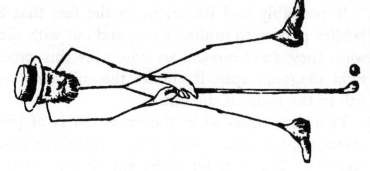

SHEER CUSSEDNESS !

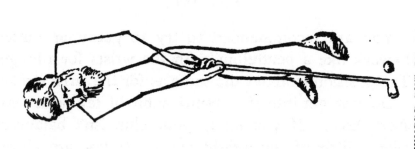

ANYWHERE BUT ON THE LINE !

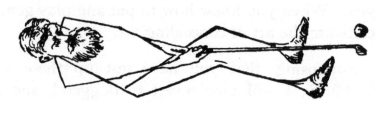

THE SLICE.

you to accompany me in one of the most singular rounds I have seen or read about. I shall disguise the players by giving them false names, and, at the the same time, for obvious reasons, I shall leave the reader to recognize, if he can, the links in their new geographical position.

TOO CLOSE TO THE BALL.

A GOOD MATCH AT ———.

F

A GOOD MATCH AT ———.

A S if the Fates had planned the strange event,
Four wandering heroes of the cleek, all bent
On golf's adventurous course, to lose or
win,
Cast anchor at Linkslochy, where the Inn
Stands out upon a corner of the links,
Whence trade is brisk in many passing drinks.

Each hero had preferred this rustic place
For his peculiar reason ; one whose grace
In spinning rhyme impelled him to retire
To homely spots where he might damp the fire
That would consume him, by the manly sport.
Another—Goffman—to this lone resort
Had come for golf, and study for a work
On all known languages from Scot to Turk.
The third—McPherson—was a man of note
Whose tastes ran wild on golf, and things remote

The fourth—one Saunders—was an ex-M.P.
Who lost his seat because he took his stand
Too often at the all-alluring tee.
And nearly lost his head, because his hand
So frequent held the pluck-inspiring brew—
A little water—lots of mountain dew !

"WHENCE TRADE IS BRISK IN MANY PASSING DRINKS."

These four, divided in all other things,
Become united in the game of swings.
A match is made, in which the man of lines
And he who to Philology inclines,
Shall play McPherson, of historic fame,
And Southern Saunders, who adores the game.

The stakes are friendly—losers have to pay
Complete expense throughout the pleasant day.

As such a chance is seldom to the fore,
To see the sport we'll watch the game, and score.

The pawky caddie makes the Saxon's tee,[1]
" Avaunt," says Saunders, "that's too weak for me."
Then from the level, off a splendid swing,
The globe becomes a very distant thing.
McPherson grins with undisguised delight,
To see the ball compelled to such a flight.
O'Connor's knowledge of his own desires,
A sudden inspiration now inspires ;
And philologic Goffman takes the lead—
(For who should start had not yet been agreed)—
The grave Teutonic nature would not vie,
As he himself, with such a prodigy :
And then again, he thought, as he could hit,
He might McPherson lure to press[2] a bit.

[1] The tee is a little mound of sand to raise the ball above the
level of the ground.
[2] To press is to play with a view to getting far, which often
causes one to play badly.

He judged aright—staid Goffman gets away—
No sign of pressing in his easy play.
O'Connor tells him why he made the change,
And Goffman answers, " Vell, but dis ist strange,
Dere's alvays limid to die bower off man!
Ich moost nicht shtrike no harder ash I can!"

But here's the ball some fifty yards behind,[1]
A truthful lie[2] to any golfer's mind ;
The caddie now explains, " Jist sic a shot
As frae the tee tae here, o' brassie-spuin,
Wad leave ye near the green or corner o't—
It's a' a cary an' ye maunae rin,
A neednae tell ye mair, Sir, for A see
Ye ken the gheme."—The ball has left the lea—
" A shplendit shtroke das ist, I vill declare!"
" Oi tipped a touch of the shilalah there!"
The two exclaim ; when in the caddie chimes,
" Weel duin, sir ! noo ye'll see as we gaun up,
That ye hae carried grund that's haurd at times,
For them that gang this gate and tak' the cup."[3]

[1] Behind the opponent's ball.
[2] A "lie" is where the ball lies.
[3] The name of a very bad bunker—a sand-pit.

McPherson on the higher ground can see
The clear approach,[1] from whins and bunkers free ;
The proper game would be the quarter cleek
Or half light iron.   But his nerve is weak,
And so the worthy Celt surprises all,
When for his putter he doth loudly call.
He's got the putter—Saunders looks a-wry—
O'Connor winks, some mischief in his eye.
But all is still, as now McPherson plays,
And all expressions change in varied ways :
For, straight, the ball careers, in bound and roll,
Till it reposes just beyond the hole.
A put of ninety yards we seldom see,
Though here the end has justified the means ;
'Tis good for trade, but golf it cannot be ;
'Twould be a failure upon most of greens.

Now as we near the hole, to our surprise,
An ugly bunker, just before it, lies ;
The cup O'Connor carried with the spoon
Is, like all dangers past, forgotten soon.

Both balls are safe upon the welcome green,[2]

[1] Approach to the hole.
[2] The space for twenty yards around the hole.

The stolid German makes a long survey,
He's marked the distance, and the line has seen
(The furthest from the hole must always play);
'Tis done most solemnly, the ball lies dead.[1]
Now Sanders puts, and bolts[2] the hole instead.
Holed out[3] in three and four.   (When balls are in
They say "holed out.")   The three's a win.

The second hole's a sporter if you like:
A streamlet at the tee, and then a dyke—
    A sloping knoll of whins
    That will punish driving sins,
Then a bunker, you may carry if you can.
    (Of course the playing round,
    On some very decent ground,
For a novice here, would be the only plan).

McPherson has the honour,[4] as we know,
But he hasn't yet decided how to go.
    Says Saunders, " Just play out
    If you feel in any doubt:

[1] So near the hole that it is sure to be put in on the next.
[2] To bolt the hole is to get it at a good pace with deadly aim.
[3] Holed out means hole finished up.
[4] Plays first.

If you'll land me near that solitary tree,
  The grass out there, I've found,
  Spreads in smoothness all around,
With a lie the hole is open[1] then to me.

McPherson is as brave as man can be,
But his bravery is tempered, as you see,
  By a caution most sublime:
  In the very nick of time,
It must save him from the worry of remorse;
  As his putter saved his nerve,
  Here a cleek shall also serve,
For he's taken Saunders' hint, and reached the course.

Now O'Connor: "Mr. Sandy, what's the play?
What's the line? and what's the carry,[2] would you say?"
  " Gin ye cautch the baa, ye'll cary,
  Ye maun keep the line—(it's nary)—
Jist straucht abun the hechest pint ye see;
  And nae hecher than it's needit,
  Gin ye want yer baa to speed it;
Syne oo maun nae mak' ye up a muckle tee."

[1] The hole is said to be open when you see a clear way to it.
[2] The carry is the distance the ball must go before touching ground.

By **the** sprig of shelalah,
Sure O'Conner's not haley,
Just the tip of the furze he did clear:
Such a ball got a lander,
Than which nothing is grander,
Eighty yards of a run,[1] never fear!

We, instinctively, follow the best driven ball,
By a path that leads up through the whins:
On the summit we stand for the far sounding call,[2]
Truly now the excitement begins.
A true rocketer shoots, with the force of despair,
From a Briton, who never gives in,
Says the caddie, " They're safe, but they'll play the
twa mair,
Gin oor baa gat nae check i' the rin."

Now we cross the fell bunker—away down the slope,
What a charming white spot we can see,
Says O'Conner, " Begorrah, they've given us rope !"
Says the Deutcher, " Ve're gut ash can pe !"

---

[1] The distance the ball runs after it has come to the ground.
[2] Golfers call out " Fore " before playing.

Another bunker tries McPherson's nerve,
He plays the cleek, for fear the club should swerve :
He's cleared the hazard, by good forty yards,
Where longer grass his further way retards.

Much thanks to brave O'Connor's perfect shot,
Now, Goffman, drive! and reach the distant
       spot!
Well done the Deutcher! if you had been straight,
The hole had been a wonder—yet 'tis great!
Within some thirty yards in two, is perfect play.
Now Sanders with the mashie gets away :
With splendid cut he cleaves the mossy grass,
And makes a stroke that nothing could surpass,
As if with sense and nerve endued, the ball
Spins well to right, from off the leftward fall.

A first class put would now secure a half ;
O'Connor's solemn : now no man may laugh.
The start is rough, his iron must stand him stead :
A supple wrist has laid him almost dead :
" O das ist gut, mein freund !" the Deutcher cries,
Some quiet excitement playing in his eyes.

McPherson, once again, must play two more ;[1]
The only chance remaining now in store
Is, if he hole, and Goffman then should fail :
So nothing but " be up "[2] can now avail.
He gives the ball a chance—by Jove it's in !
A camera ! to catch McPherson's grin !—
The Saxon's phiz !—O'Connor's look resigned !
Staid Goffman's survey of the put designed !
The leering caddies on the holed-out side !
O'Connor's Sandy, stern in Scottish pride.
And last (but more important to the play),
The player's caddie pointing out the way !

In such a moment love and care and all
Make way, most grandly, for a tiny ball ;
And now the put is played—O'Connor's face
Bespeaks the ardour of the Irish race..
He's in, in four.   As if he had been shot,
O'Connor springs two yards towards the spot,
With dashing humour seizes Goffman's hand,
And makes a bow, as funny as 'tis grand.

---

[1] Two more than the opponents have played.
[2] Be up at the hole in order to get the chance of going in.

All laugh, save Goffman, and all laugh again
To hear him solemnly, the put, explain :
" Mein freund vy all dis foos ? Iv you reflect,
To miss dat shtroke you vould not me expect."

'Tis passing strange, how character displays,
Upon the links, the secret of its ways ;
We now begin to wonder if mein freund
Is stolid from excess or want of mind.
One thing is certain, that a man like this,
If he can play, will seldom make a miss.
Golf is a game where talent leads the way,
And genius often makes unsteady play :
The reason is apparent from the fact
That little minds have little to distract.
All agitations of our thoughts reflect
Upon the game an influence direct.
The man with scarce a doubt, it is confessed,
In such a game, is sure to play his best.

Five hundred yards of sloping ground or more,
While here and there a rock, stands out before ;
When such a hill the golfer has to face,
He should not leave to chance the line or place

He means to take, but rather be content
With sure degrees, to avoid the stones and bent.
A hundred yards ahead the grass is bare,
But then some bunkered rocks and whins declare,
" The play is ' short of me,' unless you care
To try the carry, but the drive is rare ! "—

The Deutcher's doubtful what his stroke should be,
'Tis hard to play an iron off the tee.
He's not ambitious—plays the iron short.[1]

And now comes Saunders with his love of sport,
There's no mistaking his undaunted play,
Each time he takes the club he gets away.
He clears the rampart, and lies well aloft,
Where stones are scarce, and yielding grass is soft ;
O'Connor plays his ball with good address—
But Irish poets are much inclined to press—
In trying to regain advantage lost
His slice the Deutcher just a stroke, will cost.
Of course he's sorry, and begins to fret,
The stoic Goffman says, " You must forget,

[1] "Short" means playing shorter than you might do if you
wished.

Dis game, I dinks, yourself must not allow
To dink of somedingk, was ist not joost now."

The Gael who, till now, felt his hand
Just a trifle beyond his command,
    And had putted sae braw,
    For to save him a draw,
Doth his old heavy driver, demand.

With a grin, most suggestive of wit,
He explains, " It will help us a bit ! "
    And without any press—
    To O'Connor's distress—
He has made a magnificent hit.

    " By the powers ! " thinks O'Connor,
    " 'Twill be small dishonour
If we don't beat such devils as they,
    For I never saw playin'
    Betoken more stayin' !
Sure the worst that can happen, is pay ! "

A slice of luck !—The ball is lying clear,
Though rocks around, and whins are very near.

The placid Goffman's ball finds quick relief;
The lofting iron has modified the grief
The Irish spirit's up—we know it well—
As many a doughty warrior can tell;
It gives full courage, unsuspected might—
It gives the backward ball a wond'rous flight
To climb the hill, and run along the top
Some fifty yards beyond the favouring hop.
A good two more!   Anticipation keen
Now speculate the chance of " on the green."
We may not hurry—Meinherr Goffman won't—
Although the others now are well in front.

Observe this well!   No curious instinct pries
To know exactly where O'Connor lies.
A thorough golfer's thoughts must never roam;
He, like the miser, keeps them all for home;
So Saunders takes the cleek, and proves that he,
With every tool, has gained dexterity.

McPherson now plays to O'Connor, the like[1]—
For the latter is up past the line of the dyke—

[1] The like is when a like number of strokes have been played
on either side.

The half from the iron again is the game,
Though a full with the mashie might do.
We detect here a weakness—in many the same—
Golfing knowledge is mastered by few !—
So up goes the mashie, away goes the ball,

"IN COOLING GLADES."

But it lofts a bit short, with no run on at all ;
And now we may hope (as may plainly be seen,
If the Deutcher plays well)—for a fight on the green.

Herr Goffman exhibits, as we might expect,
An absence of wrist-work, so hard to correct :
His great heavy body and wit are combined

G

To play as they can, and give sport to the wind :
But with all, he's a stunner at judging the roll,[1]
For he's sent in a ball that may save them the hole.

Now Saunders, in putting, is deadly and true ;
He must give it a chance, yet avoid the run thro'—[2]
It looks easy enough, just to play and lie dead ;
But it's easier still to lie living instead—
The adept has played with his wonted decision,
His ball is laid near and they play for division ;[3]
O'Connor gets in with a put of six feet.
The match is still even.   The game is a treat !

*   *   *   *   *   *

The scene is lovely, if we look around
(But Golfers' eyes are mostly on the ground),
Away to south and east fair Sylvia reigns
Among the varied charms of wide domains.
The tints of Autumn here and there display
Harmonious contrast with the brown and grey—
The clumps of larch, all sleeping in the sun,
Invite the dogs, and tempt the ready gun.

[1] Run or travel.
[2] Run through means run past the hole with too much force.
[3] Division of this hole.

In cooling glades, along the limpid stream,
The ruminators rest, as in a dream ;
On verdant lawn the independent lamb
Asserts its freedom, and forsakes the dam—

"LO ! THE MIGHTY SEA."

All—all is past the pleasant summer bloom—
The golden wheat awaits an early doom :—
And see ! beyond this lowland Paradise
The purple hills in multitude arise,
Where drowsy mists and fleecy clouds betray
The universal stillness of the day.

The eye may wander in sweet exercise
Some fifty miles where mountains meet the skies—
Then turn around, and, lo! the mighty sea
Of green and blue—superb in majesty.
One tiny murmur, on the silver sand,
In rhythmic cadence, breaks the silent spell,
Where, in the storm, great rollers sweep the land
And build the varied links we love so well.

For the next we must now get away.
All even[1] and fifteen to play—
   This tee you've been told
   Is a sight to behold
For the ball has to carry a bay.

From the hill, some two hundred feet high,
With trees and a precipice nigh—
   An arm of the brine
   Lying right in your line—
You may clear if you're willing to try.

[1] All even in holes.

Our good friend of no " Blitzen und donner "
To drive the last hole had the honour,[1]
    So now do we know
    That the critical blow
Must be tried by the supple O'Connor.

He will take the straight line, I'll be bound,
An Irishman never goes round,
    " Nae pressin' ava,
    Keep yer ee on the baa,"
Says the caddie, preparing the ground.

At this hole, it is something to see
A good ball fly away from the tee ;
    When out in mid-air,
    You begin to despair,
And you think you'll go into the sea.

O'Connor the creek has well cleared,
Where the hole, off a cleek, may be neared ;
    McPherson's A1 ;

[1] The winners of the last hole or game have the honour—to play first from the tee.

For his ball isn't done,
By a good running loft,[1] he is cheered.

They hole out[2] in four on each side,
So it counts, as you know, a divide.
    The next tee is ready,
    The Deutcher, so steady,
A minute just takes to decide.

No. 5 requires judgment and skill;
For the course runs along by the hill,
    And it slopes to the sand
    Where it's easy to land,
So you play to the left with good will.

But if you should draw[3] by mischance,
You're undone, you may see at a glance;
    For the top of the knoll,
    Like a green headed poll,
Would defy all the barbers in France.

---

[1] Running loft means a ball pitching on ground that helps it forward.

[2] Finish the hole.

[3] Draw the stroke so as to make the ball go to the left of the line intended.

Herr Goffman has hit very well ;
But the slope gives him running so fell
     He careers o'er the land
     And gets down on the strand,
While O'Connor ejaculates—" Well ! "

Saunders now is the next to play off—
He's a wonderful master of Golf—
     He's away in a trice,
     With a terrible slice [1]
As if at all danger to scoff.

He has skimmed away out very low—
Gets the rise when the whins are below,
     Then he soars to full height
     And goes round to the right
Like the ugliest ball that we know.

O'Connor the odd [2] has to play,
With the niblick the ball gets away.

---

[1] A ball hit so as to curve to the right from the line of aim is said to be sliced.

[2] A stroke more than has been played by the opponents.

The Deutcher's two more ·
May secure them a four ;
But a lose is as clear as the day.

· For Saunders had judged it so well,
And his ball had such spin when it fell,
    That it took the incline
    With a curve on its line
And was nearly hole high[1] in the dell.

Each face agitation bespoke—
'Twas a feat of true skill and no joke !—
    They might have holed out
    In the second no doubt,
But McPherson was short on his stroke.

Excitement keeps too much alive
The Golfer's nerve to put and drive,
'Tis often thus a three and four
Is followed by a double score.

Both sides at No. 6. are bad—
    O'Connor's left the course—

---

[1] Up to the hole.

McPherson finds the bunker sad,
   Because he used such force—
The Deutcher, ever most resigned,
   Gets out from prickly whins,
Remarking now, " Mein younger friend
   Exzitment zeldom vins,
You spare die nerfs, you sblendit play !
   Dink nod off nodingk past,
You bardon me, I know die vay
   To vin dis match ad last.
Iv you poot blay die quiet game
   McPherson vill nod to it—
Die Keltic race ist all de zame,
   Und ovedendimes dey rue it !"

"Bedad," says O'Connor, "you've spoken the truth,
   The greatest defect in me game
Is a fullness of thought I have known from me youth ;
   It wants some correction—that same !"

   "You dry to dink oopon die shot
     You blay, und how to blay it,

Und alvays vatch die ferry spot
 Vereon die cloob you lay it ! "

This hole in seven they divide ;
 And seven too, in fives ;
While eight is four on either side—
 At nine good Saunders drives.

The last two holes were free from care,
 For hazards were but few ;
But No. 9's une autre affaire,
 No slice or draw will do.

The hole is short—now Saunders plays
 A neat three-quarter[1] loft :
His under-cut[2] the ball delays
 On green so smooth and soft.

Old Goffman recks not hazards round,
 He gauges Saunder's strength ;
The full three-quarters reached the ground,
 His full might give the length.

[1] See instructions for explanation.
[2] Back spin on the ball.

The Deutcher's shrewd,
His judgment's good,
The full iron brings him up—
As we go near,
By Jove how queer,
He's almost in the cup!

This hole explains
How settled brains,
With method, must be used.
Methodic pluck
Is crowned by luck,
Where science is refused.

The hole is perfect, 2 and 3
Makes even at the turn : [1]
O'Connor scarce restrains his glee
And now they face the burn.

The 10th, 11th, 12th, divide ;
In 4 then 6 then 5 aside ;
But at the 13th, Goffman heels, [2]

[1] The turn to come home.   Half the round of eighteen holes.
[2] Or slices, go to the right of the intended line.

While Saunders once again reveals
A tidy drive along the straight—
Two hundred yards at any rate.

Another lesson here we find,
In playing golf with hand and mind.
O'Connor's out some eighty yards,
And Goffman's ball the green rewards.
McPherson has begun to wonder,
" How in all ta name off Thunder
A foreign person plays like zat
Whatever too he's also fat,
An I so thin can't do as well ! "—
And on his nerve it works a spell,
A good half iron is the thing,
But he can only do the swing.
His iron full would take him past—
    The mashie would be short—
He hesitates—decides at last :
    The putter's his resort.
He plays it well, but sundry bumps
    Betray the anxious putter ;
From knoll to knoll, zig-zag, he thumps
    And makes his partner mutter,

" By Jingo that's a funny swipe
McPherson's surely fond of snipe ;
I cannot think, in all creation,
Of any better imitation ! "

But worst of all the pent-up ire,
Though well controlled, will not expire :
And hands will never work at golf
When such high steam wants letting off—
No inconsistent swearing came
To calm the nerve or quench the flame.

Saunders has placed him very near ;
    O'Connor's lying dead in four ;
McPherson plays his put, in fear
    Lest he should miss—has run it o'er—
The patient Saunders leads the way :
    All even still and five to play.

The 14th hole is very short,
    Within a tiny glade ;
But whins and bunkers yield the sport.
    (It must be neatly played).

It's just the awkward stroke between
   A quarter and a half:
In raising which, to reach the green,
   So many raise a laugh— .

'Twas Sandy planned Linkslochy links
   To foster art and science,
For every kind of stroke, he thinks,
   On which we place reliance
     "Comes in the plaun
     To try oor haun
At Gowfer's true preceesion,
    There's aye a roun'
    For ony loon
That has nae that deceesion."

   Now at this hole
   One must control
The Club, to take the distance :
   A stroke too short
   Through whins must sport,
A long one's no assistance.
A perfect green of forty yards

A master of the loft regards
  As ample space for travel :
Then he who does not take delight
In such a loft, may play to right,
Then enter as a lady might,
  Which leaves no ground for cavil.

O'Connor's nimble wrist has found,
With ease, the grateful putting ground :
And now McPherson spares a swing—
A hybrid shot—a foolish thing ;
His judgment of the strength is great ;
But such a stroke is seldom straight :
Ten yards to left, eighteen too. far,
The chances of the hole will mar.

Saunders is true, but rather gay ;
The ball has run two yards away,
And now the student of the mind,
Whose ball is eight good yards behind,
With clever palm upon the lea,
He tests its elasticity.
He will not risk, though all is clear,
With steady put, he runs it near :

Our brave McPherson feels that he
Would rather storm a battery.
The lack of confidence comes in,
But not the ball, to save a win.
They finish up in three and four—
One up and four to play the score.

The 15th hole is halved in six—
    The course a gentle slope—
But now the next is full of tricks,
    With which the play must cope:
Before the tee a running stream,
Where crystal waters idly dream,
    In shimmering beams of light ;
And out beyond, upon the rise,
A bunker of unusual size,
    Inviting, greets the sight.

Each ball, with dire decision's hit,
And sallies of congenial wit
    Around the party scatter ;
But when they come a stroke to play
The wit yields up its jocund sway—
    The stroke's a serious matter.

Hallo there !—Goffman's stroke is bad—
  And now at last he's laughing :
" Exguse me I vill not pe sad
  Because die pall I'm baffing,
I shoost have put you far enough,
  Die next vill reach die pottingk :
Die spirits ve must nefer rough—
  You drive him home like nodingk."

Good Saunders makes a lovely try,
  But cannot reach the goal.
O'Connor's got a pretty lie
  Much nearer to the hole—
A thorough demon on the line,
  He now consults his caddie ;
" Come, Sandy, if you've got a min
  You'll help this Irish Paddy ! "

" Odds, sir, ye've just to tak the spuin—
Yill min' yon shot at No yin—
The distance an' the lie's the same—
An easy drive 'll tak ye hame."

H

His spirit's up for anything—
To save the hole his ball takes wing.
O'Connor cries, " Well, there is luck !"
" No," says the German, " 'tis die pluck ! "

McPherson plays a little wide :
Lo ! now the balls are side by side.

A foot apart—a perfect stimie laid,[1]
May bring new trouble ere the hole is played.

They lie the like ;[2] does Goffman like the lie ?—
He'll try the stroke that nerves must surely try.

That stroke may be very imperfect in grace,
But it lays the ball dead, in a very good place :
It was right as to line, but was checked in the roll,
And it stimies the ball that's away from the hole.

It is hard upon Saunders, who might have got in :
He must play up with care, and relinquish a win.

[1] A stimie is laid when you have the opponent's ball between
you and the hole.
[2] As to the number of strokes.

The game is now 1 up and 2 to play
Next hole—the longest we have seen to-day—
Most men for distance here incline to press ;
But Goffman has his plan—he won't digress,
Now drives the Saxon with enormous strength,
As if in one fell stroke he'd reach the length.
A marvel that indeed !—the ball starts low,
And skims the ground for eighty yards, or so,
Then, unexpectedly, begins to rise—
Then soars aloft, and meets the sunny skies.

Now brave O'Connor—every muscle strained—
Plays up the odds against the advantage gained—
In famous style, an arrow's line he takes,
And on the opponent ninety yards he makes.

The grand McPherson casts his coat aside,
To help the pace—for this may well decide
This hole momentous.   Longer drivers here,
With equal skill, are certain first to near
The distant flag, which in the end implies
An almost certain gain ; but fate defies,
At awkward times, the hope so prone to rise
For Golf is like all human enterprise.

At last the green is reached in 4 and 6,
O'Connor's ball is dead—we like such tricks.
Now steady, Saunders! you have two to win !—
That put is perfect, but—oh luck unkind !
Your ball has swerved—it knocks O'Connor in,
While you to play the like are left behind.

Holed out in 6 apiece makes dormey 1,[1]
O'Connor's phiz bespeaks the latent fun,
But looking round he finds in Goffman's face,
Of fun or humour, not the slightest trace.
And stern McPherson, with a dire intent,
Revolves the chances of the great event.
Like to a hero of the olden time
Prepared against all odds—he looks sublime !
While Saunders, until now unmoved by aught,
Confounds the luck with which this game is fraught.

This hole is just what 18th holes should be,
To test the nerve and prove dexterity.

[1] Dormey means, as many holes ahead or "up" as there are holes to play. Very comfortable, as it is impossible to lose. I fancy the spelling would be more traditional as " Dormez."

One hundred yards away, a tinkling brook
Meanders down the undulating vale,
Its distant murmurs, heard in many a nook,
Upon the stillness of the air prevail.
The slope is steeper on the further side,
And out beyond the course is smooth and wide ;
Then bunkers by no drive as yet attained—
When over these a clear play home is gained.

O'Connor you're in clover,
For your nature would run over,
If your partner ceased to school you with a frown.
Than you no man is gayer
As a very pretty player,
But your fretting and delighting keep you down.

O'Connor to his caddie :
" Now instruct me, my good laddie,
For I leave my own and take your good advice. "
And the caddie to O'Connor:
" Dinnae press and spoil the honour
O' a roond A wudnae loss at ony price.

" Jist see the tee is tae yer mind—
An easy swing—a stroke that's kind
   'Ll laund ye ower !
A wee bit free 'll clear the brink,
An tak ye faurer than ye think
  'Thoot muckle power !

" Ye'll easy reach the green in three—
   In twa ye cannae mack it ;
Sae tak this kindly, Sir, frae me—
   Yer back ye maun nae rack it !

" An' mind yer ee, yer wits an a'—
   Forget the rest—
They maun be fixed upon the baa'
   An dinnae press't ! "

O'Connor goes off like a ball from a gun,
And he's over the glen with a very good run—
McPherson has pressed—like a demon he flew,
For he saw that, to win, they must drive it in two.
His caddie's not hopeful of making a save—
As he crosses the glen, he is looking so grave;
And if we could hear him addressing his chum,
I think this is nearly to what it would come :—

McPHERSON'S CADDIE.

" Ma certie, Sandy isnae blate—
 He's gotten brains !—
Or may be Goffman set 'm tae't,
 An' for 'is pains
He's countin' on the clink o' gless,
 An' bonny aets ;
An' mair than a'—tae ma distress—
 He'll wun the bates.
A ne'er jaloused but Airish chiels
 Could wrax a wrung,
They're aye sae ready, i' the biels,
 Wi' wag o' tongue.
But wha'd a thocht this chiel sae braw
 Wad play sae bonny :
He dangs the deil, wi' club an baa',
 As guid as ony."

SAUNDERS'S CADDIE.

" Aweel ! Aweel maun, dinnae faush
    Oor luck's ben awfu' sair,
Ye've wagered, gin ye lose yer caush,
    Syne, muckle care."

The stereotypic Goffman plays the odd—
Nor dreams of foozle[1] on the lovely sod.
McPherson's neck-or-nothing but rewards
The foolish risk with ten or twenty yards,
And, after all, as Saunders is aware
Of all his partner's weakness in the game,
To get him forward he may hardly dare,
Because at doubtful distance he is tame.
Poor Saunders—most polite—assumes the lie,
Is very doubtful—plays three quarters high,
In order that McPherson by good chance,
And driving full, their prospect may advance.

O'Connor with his brassie plays again—
Again he's reached the much requested plain,

[1] Missing the stroke.

Now drives McPherson—just across the green—
That Saunders knows his game, is clearly seen.

But now the struggle comes—that awful hole—
The final put, in vain we would control.
The Deutcher plays on this occasion full ;
His lie was bad—as lies are as a rule;
Three yards at least beyond the magic ring,
In keen suspense, awaiting anything.

Saunders has counted up the chances fine,
His lie is awkward too, for strength and line—
A knoll, in front, that we negotiate,
To keep the line, may well affect the rate.
He plays—but dead, his ball will not remain—
McPherson now by yards can measure pain.
O'Connor's put, by nervous twitch restrained,
Drew up too soon, and three feet short remained.
Now proud McPherson ! by thine ancient clan,
Claymores and sporans ! prove yourself a man !
Throw nervous care aside and hole the ball ;
If you can do as you have often done,
'Twill make all right for neither shall have won !
He does his best, but oh ! that horrid lip !
The curling ball disdains the trifling dip.

The Deutcher still must hole—his nerve is cool—
He's not the kind of man that plays the fool—
All hope for Saunders and McPherson's done—
The hole is halved in six—the match is won!

The Dreadful will give hole—his drive is cool—
He's not the kind of man that play the fool—
All hope for Sanders and McPherson's done—
The hole is halved in six—the match is won.

SANDY COW'S FUNERAL

SANDY GOW'S FUNERAL.

BY ONE OF THE CADDIES WHO CARRIED HIM
TO THE GRAVE.

UIR Sandy Gow's[1]
  Gaen ower the knowe,
The hindmost bunker's ta'en um ;
  The stanes sae high
  Aroond his lie
A'm shuir frae gowf'll spane um.

  He's in a hole
  He can nae thole,
He's ghie an' sair forfuchen,
  An whan tha blast
  Caus up at last

[1] The writer may be accused of a spelling that violates all the conventionalities, but the fact that Broad Scotch is badly pronounced even among Scotchmen in recent times will justify phonetics.

The keeng, the duke, an' cauddie,
    A's warr'nt he'll
    Hissell reveal
A worthy gowfin' lauddie.

    A week sin syne
    He gan tae tyne—
(Eh, man, A didnae like it),—
    A passed the nicht
    Tae see um richt
Whar he was cosey beikit.

    Says he, " Man John,
    The time weers ohn,
An' life is growin' dreary,
    A'm gaun awa'
    Whar cleek an baw
An' bunkered links are cheery ! "
    Od sake, his words
    Neer turned tae curds
The bluid in ilka vein, man,
    A took a drahm,
    To stimie quam,
Whan he began again, man.

"Man John," says he,
As wake's could be,
"A'm shuir tae gang tae Heeven,
For I hae seen   -
The bonny green
The menisters believe in ;
The ither nicht
Whan A was richt—
It wus nae dream, A'm thinkin—
A saw a licht
Fornent ma sicht—
A thocht A hud bin drinkin'.

"An then A minded A was deed,
But aye the licht was lowie :
It was na eerie—A could dree'd,
An didnae feel that dowie.
An' syne A saw 'ithin the lowe
A bonny Aungel lauddie,
Says he 'Cu wah across the knowe
Ye'll hae me for a cauddie."
Says I, 'A's rather tak tha' heel
Ye'll play, an A'll e'en cary.'

'Na na,' says he, 'the laund o' leal
    Is whar ye're gaun tae tary!
It's written i' the jidgement buik
    Thit Sandy Gow's eleckit,
Fur tho' the Bible he forsaik,
    Tha Saubath he respeckit.
It's true, it say's, thit whiles he drank
    A guid drap o' the whuskey—
He aye bood doon tae men o' raunk
    An' was nae prood or busky ;
His thochts were a' for play an' gowf,
    An' whiles a wee bit sweerin'—
He couldnae pairt frae drucken howf
    Tho faur the nicht was weerin'.
He robbed his faither o' a cleek,
    An' napped his brither's wages,
An' managed a' sae braw an' sleek
    It wusnae kent for ages.
But he may thaunk his mither's sect,
    For through her soft protection
He could nae miss—by faith elect—
    Salvation's competition.
Sae noo ye're gaun tae'e laund o' leal
    Get oot yer clubs an' baw, man !

For sixty years ye've carried weel !
  Ye've haen nae sport ava', man.'
A syne poodoot ma rig, an' soft
  He slang thum ower his shoother,
An' syne we baith gaed faur aloft
  As tho' oo's blaun wi' poother.

" Man John, the links wus graun, nae doot,
  Bit jist as A wus swingin'
A gied the muin an awfu' cloot,
  The din like thunner ringin' :
Wi' that tha veeshn brocht me bauck,
  An' left me sairly faushit,
Ye'll no believe me, buit its fauck,
  A broke oor biggest auchet."

    A humlin sicht
    That awfu' nicht
Was puir auld Gow sae feckit ;
    He wad reveal
    The land o' leal
Wi' clubs an' bunkers deckit.
    The oors glode by
    Till in the sky

The bonny sun wus shinin',
   Than, " John," says he,
   " A'm gaun tae dee,
A feel ma force is tinin',
   Ye micht rin doon
   Toe'e preachin' loon
An' aux 'm tae come heer, man :
   A gosp'l chiel
   Suid ken fu' weel,
O dathe tae check oor feer, man."

Up at the maunse wi' a ma speed
   A' sweng the sonsy knocker.
The preacher, syne, pits oot aes heed,
   Jist fresh frae Murphy's locker.
A' tells 'm hoo auld Sandy Gow
Is thenkin' shuin the gress 'll grow
   Abain aes bodey ;
An' thaen the minister tae me ;
" A' trust, man Scott, it's no thit he's
   B'n drenkin' Toddy ! "
" Na ! na ! it is nae drink," says I ;
" Than, wait," says he ; " A'll gang ower by
   This very meenit ;

"THE PREACHER, SYNE, PITS OOT AES HEED."

Bit mind an' wait, for in the glen
Ye'll easy tell me a' ye ken
O' Sandy's life in Lochy Glen
    Ye maun hae seen it."

A' telt 'm as oo daundered doon
Thit Saundy wus nae sic a loon
But whan 'ae wager'd hauf a croon
    He'd hae the siller,
Hoo a' his life, upone the links,
Wus gowf be day, be nicht the drinks,
An' hoo in curlin' time his rinks
    Aye bate the Miller.

An' hoo hees cariers flew sae faust
He could nae git a mautch et laust,
An' hoo his life hud awe bin paust
    Wi' ghemme an' drenken.
The minister wus gaie an' blate,
Nae doot ae thocht, bit wud nae say 't,
" Repentance never comes too late "
    As A wus thinkin'.
Than frae'es pooch the Bible taen
Tae search for texts thit micht explain

The knotey pints thit sic a swain
  Wad likely mention.
He lookit raither mair than fractious
Aboot thaut fleein'-pegeon practice,
He could nae finnd a text tae act es
  Antedot'l.
An' aence aw heerd um i' the kirk
Declare thit whusky wus a dirk
That steekit sowls thit loo the mirk :
  (He wus teetot'l).

Syne Sandy's hoose,
Wi' thocht sae croose,
  Oo reached fu' shuin.
A lift the sneck
'Thoot muckle feck,
  An' we gang enn.

Tho' Sandy's rin wus nearly check't
  He tell'd wi' grete preceesh'n—
(Whiles stoppin' thaut he micht reflect)—
  The minister his veesh'n.

Thaen syne says he,
"D'ye thenk thit we
May finned a links in Heeven,
Or whut'll dae
Up there tae play?
Tell me whut ye believe en!";

"A dinnae ken," tha preacher says,
"If gowf's a gheme immort'l,
For in the future nae maun's gaze
Has gote ayont the port'l:
I'll search the scripture ower again
An' finnd if there is menshn
O' faucks that micht wi' gowfin' men
Relate to your contenshn:
Buit, fore the rest ye may be shuir
Thur's awthing there thit's bonny,
The pow'r tae leave for ever mair
Wi' ilka faithfu' cronnie:
Gin we believe then we shaull live
But gin we doot we digh!"
Syne Saundy, "A' believe abuive
There's gowfin' i' the sky!"

Tha Minister wus fickled there:
'Twus plain that Saundy kent nae mair:
An' straucht ae tried tae press a wee
Tae let thae puir auld boddy see
Afore he shuid exauckly dee
 The promised laun'.
He telt 'm hoo aw things agree,
An' hoo th' elect wi' speerits free
Wad a' be hauppy ez could be
 Wi' aung'l baun'.

"Is't true, than, Minister," says Gow,
"Thit A'wm gaun hame tae there enow?"
"Gin ye believe ye're justified,
But gin ye doot ye'll be denied."

But noo auld Saundy's senkin' faust,
An' ilka brathe micht be tha laust.
A sudd'n licht glints enn his ee;
"E'st true thit a' the aungels flee?"

"Oo, aye, aw angl's flee, forby
Oo'll aw hae wings tae soar on high."

" An' wull oo ken ilk ither there,
Whan awthing looks sae braw an' fair ? "

" Oo, aye, oo'll ken, an' you an' me
'Ll meet up there as shuir's a' dee ! "

    " Oo daurnae hae oor Driver ? "

" Na ! na ! ye maun nae faush they things,   .
Oo'll be like aungels wi' oor wings—"

    " A'll flee ye for a fiver ! ! ! "

The minister stood up tae pray
    Some blessin' on his heed ;
Buit a' thit ahy could thenk or say
    Wus, " Saundy Gow lies deed ! "
    *   *   *   *

Oor a' jist in a plash o' sweet,
    You've caried wi' a wull,
There's Airchie Thamson's ower the street,
    Oo'll gang an' hae a jull !

August 16th, 1894.

"A'LL FLEE YE FOR A FIVER !"

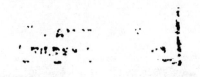

RULES OF THE GAME.

RULES OF THE GAME.

I.

HO' every side must have a ball,
The ball should never have a side,
The sides consist of two or more
Who play as other rules decide.

II.

2

To play the game you take your tee
And place your ball upon it,
And drive it off towards the hole,
And play until you've done it.
Each stroke you make is counted well
Until the hole's completed,
The smaller number wins the hole :
The greater is defeated.

[1] The marginal numbers refer to the St. Andrews Rules in
their original order.

Though equal numbers halve the point,
   Great numbers have it rarely,
And often when we have the hole
   We hate to halve it fairly !

III.

3 The ground for tee—oft marked by ells—
   (To which the course is vertical),
Two clubs in width, from front to back,
   Makes everything symmetrical ;
And if you tee outside of this
   Opponents may recall—
No matter how you may protest
   You drive another ball.
N.B. The hole has a mouth as the course keeper
     knows,
   Just four and a half inches wide ;
But it should not have lips that might lead us to
     blows,
   That may rob of a win, or divide.

IV.

4 If you move your club with intention to strike,
   A stroke it will always cost ;

If you push, or scoop, if you scrape or the like,
 The hole is (for certain) lost.
So if it's a game you'd have luck at,
The ball must be honestly struck at.

V.

5 The game is begun by the sides striking off
 From the first teeing ground we all know,
Then partners alternately play at the tee,
 And the whole of each hole as they go.
The sides, when commencing, arrange who's to
  play
 From the first teeing ground, and from thence
The order's maintained for the whole of the match,
 If you play out of turn its immense ;
6 For example, a play out of turn at the tee,
 An opponent the stroke may recall ;
But away from the tee such an error, you'll find,
 Will just cost you a hole.   That is all !

VI.

9 When the balls have left the tee,
 Then you carefully must see

K

Which is furthest from the hole you have in view,
 For that ball must always play,
 Though the other lead the way
 (Save where more than two essay,
When in such a case impediments won't do);
 Should the wrong side play the ball
 An opponent may recall,
Ere his side has played the ball that follows you.

- VII.

10 When you've teed and driven off,
 In the noble game of golf,
You must never touch your ball without consent;
 If it's touched or changed or moved,
 Then the penalty is proved,
You must lose a stroke and try to be content.
13 When the hole is finished out,
 You may lift the ball no doubt,
And also if it's sticking in a fen,
 Or a most unlucky loft,
 Where the soil or sand is soft,
Just to loosen it, and drop it in again.

VIII.

12 If in long grass or near a bush
　　　　Your ball should lie,
　　You neither bend nor break nor push,
　　　　Nor ever try
　　To move a growing or fixed thing away,
　　Your only licence is address and play :
　　That is, you may but footing find secure,
　　Then sole your club and play or else endure
　　The forfeit of the hole, unless the ball
18　　Be hidden from your view : then you may bend
　　Enough to let you see it—that is all !
　　　　No matter what direction it may trend.

IX.

28　Though seldom missed a ball is often lost,
　　And this by strictest rule the hole will cost.
　　Five minutes are allowed, the search begun,
　　When time is up the opponent's hole is won.

X.

29　A ball must be played from wherever it lies,
　　　　Except where the rules make provision,

Though you maul for a month without making it
    rise,
  Or the loss of the hole's the decision.

XI.

36   ·On the green or where you like,
    If your ball the other strike,
Your opponent may replace or let it stay ;
    And then comes the little joke
    That he does not count a stroke,
If you hole him out to help him on his way.
    Then again a stroke you lose,
    Very simply if you choose,
But to play your ball before the other rest.
    There's some knowledge of the mind
    In this trifling rule defined,
For a good one's hard to follow at the best.

XII.

37   If by word or look or motion
    Is conveyed the slightest notion,
Saving by the caddies or the sides,
    And you knowingly have played on ·

Such advice the forfeit's laid on
" Lose the hole," this canon soon decides.

XIII.

40   If a subject of contention
Call for outside intervention
Then the players may appoint a referee,
But if either take objection,
And the players on reflection
Fail to clear the matter up or to agree,
Either side may then refer it
For decision on its merit
To the Green Committee of that special Club.
And this rule hath made provision
That those gentlemen's decision,
Shall be final as the chances of a rub.
Should the point in dispute not be covered by rules
Then the arbitors equity follow,
And however inclined to consider them fools
Their prescription you're destined to swallow.

XIV.

38   If the ball while you're in play
Take to cracking by the way,

Or unplayable become from any flaw,
  Your opponent you apprise
  And another, where it lies,
May replace it without contravening law.
  If in halves the ball should fly—
  Pieces equal to the eye—
Either half you may supplant it is agreed,
  But when the globule splits
  And becomes unequal bits,
You replace the largest portion and proceed.

XV.

8   A round of Links here makes a match,
  So by the links you're chained
Unless before the game begins
  A special game's ordained,
Whichever side gets holes a-head
  Beyond the holes remaining,
Or wins the last when that before
  Made, '*even*' one for gaining,
    The rules maintain
    The match doth gain ;

The match is halved if at the last
No side ahead can number,
But this is clear without details
Which heads and tales encumber.

XVI.

11   If within a club length of your ball,
Loose impediments go to the wall,
But that which, than a club length is more,
To remove will add one to your score.
But this rule does not serve very much
If a hazard you happen to touch
The condition's precise,
Although not very nice.
You may forfeit the hole for your pains,
For there's nothing but glass
They've consented to pass
Should you batter with cobbles your brains.

XVII.

14   If the ball's in a hazard or touching the same
Not a thing must you touch ere you strike,

Your sole right is to footing for playing the game,
 The forfeit's the hole,
 Your nerves pray control
For its odd when your playing the like.

XVIII.

15   A hazard is a bunk
 You may find in any Bunker
 Where man is sure to funk
 If he be at all a funker;
 Here you have a list of some
 That will never make your summer :
 Water, Sand, or ditches dumb,
 Loose earth and mole-hills dumber,
 Roads and Railways simple both,
 Rabbit scrapes and fences bother.
 Rushes, Bushes—nothing loth
 To make any man a lother,
 Then the everlasting whin
 That prevents the ardent winner,
 If you never knew a sin,
 That, perchance, will make a sinner.
 Whatever there is strange

Or to the course a stranger.
Exceptions :—sands that range
When wind has been the arranger,
Then sand upon the grass
T' improve a part that's crasser,
And snow or ice so crass
Bare patches upon grass, Sir.
A hazard is a mess
Awaiting golfing Messrs!
How often no egress
When we become digressors!

XIX.

16 Of all the errors of some ardent souls
No simpler can we have for losing holes,
When we have left the ever welcome tee
If slight protuberance we chance to see
Unto our ball in close proximity
We gently tread it, just to make it plain
The hole is lost—whatever else we gain.
And mark this well—an ever salient fact—
Your caddie or yourself may do the act.

XX.

21　　If in water you lie or be lost,
　　　　You may drop a ball back on the lea
　　One stroke this performance will cost—
　　　　Drink is awkward in golf all agree.

XXI.

17　　If upon the course a barrow,
　　　　Tool or roller, box or harrow,
　　Machine, or such obstruction in the way,
　　　　Embarrass you in playing,
　　　　Then it follows, without saying,
　　You're entitled to remove it as you may :
　　But if a ball should rest upon or touch
　　　　Analogous obstructions, nets or clothes,
　　It may be lifted (for the rule is such)
　　　　And then dropped upon the sward
　　　　Without forfeit or reward,
　　　　To save the ready effluence of oaths.

　　Yet if these circumstances come to pass
　　　In any hazard, then the globe must fall

Prone in the hazard where it was, alas !
Too much good luck would spoil the game for all.

Then again, if you lie in a golf hole,
Or a hole that a flag-staff has shaped,
Lift and drop—but not more than a club length,
And behind the said hole you've escaped.

XXII.

19 The player, when allowed to drop a ball,
Himself alone achieves the important fall ;
Behind the hazard he must stand erect—
As far behind it as he may elect—
The spot from which he lifted ; or, in case
He entered water, then, the diving-place—
Th' unfinished hole and he must all be lined
When from his head he drops the ball behind.

XXIII.

20 When balls in play lie very near,
Their nearest points we measure ;
And if there's not six inches clear,
The playing side, at pleasure,

May then remove th' opponent's ball,
　　Play on, and then replace it.
But, if the lifting move at all
　　Your ball and you can trace it,
　　　　You have the right,
　　　　As well you might,
To put it back to play at.
　　　　And then again
　　　　'Tis very plain
The lie the other lay at
　　　　May be deranged,
　　　　Or slightly changed,
When you the stroke are making :
　　　　In such a case
　　　　Th' opponents claim
　　　　Another place
　　　　That is the same
Near what they are forsaking.

XXIV.

22　If a ball while in motion should happen to strike
　　(Though it could not well strike without motion)
A fore caddie, a horse, or a cart, or the like,
　　Or a gull sailing in from the ocean,

Or by accident change in its course from a cause
   That is outside the match it is played in,
'Tis a rub of the green as defined by the laws,
   And it's played from the lie it is laid in.

If a ball take a fancy to ride in a dray,
   Or where it might find locomotion,
Then that ball or another must drop for the play
   Without a degrade or promotion ;
Which means, if recovered, you drop it as near
   As you can where the passing obstruction
Was moving or standing when in it the ball
First was lodged : and of course it is perfectly clear
   That the rule would be foolish instruction
      Unless we might use
      A new ball if we choose,
      Though the other we cannot recover at all.
      For, as Paddy might say,
      " The ball couldn't be lost
      If you knew it must lay
      In a cart of loose hay,
      That you couldn't get tossed,
     Or a sheep hurried off to destruction."

Then finally, a ball at rest
Removed from where it lay
By agency outside the match,
May be replaced for play.
If on the course, it must be dropped ;
But if it's on the green
The ball may be replaced by hand,
As most of us have seen.

XXV.

23   If a side or what belongs to it in caddie or in club
Touch the other's ball in motion it will never
count a " rub."
The penalty's decidedly the losing of the hole,
And if you've had a stinger your opponent may
condole.

The selfsame penalty's imposed if, when the ball's
at rest,
By accident yourself or yours remove it from its
nest.
24   Again this penalty comes in if, in a single stroke,
You give your ball a double tap, although it seems
a joke.

The penalty, it seems to me,
The stroke and not the hole should be
  (At least upon the course),
For when you hit this kind of twin
'Tis cruel as some recoiling sin !
  The stroke's devoid of force ! !
Once more this horrid penalty th' opponent's
    side will claim,
  If while thy ball's in motion it but touch or
    thee or thine.
Thy partner, clubs, or caddie, or whatever has a
    name,
  And is capable of influence upon the speed or
    line.

XXVI.

25 If a side, its clubs, or caddies, when the ball has
      left the tee,
  Touch and change its ball's position, it shall pay
      the penalty.
        It isn't so much
        For a very slight touch,
  Just a stroke and the side may go free.

XXVII.

26 Now the meaning of touching and moving the
   ball
      Must be fixed by a clear definition.
   If you only touch it or move it at all,
      And it rests in some other position,
   It is moved ; but, if aimed at, it swing to and fro,
      And where first it was found it reposes,
   Highly pleased with your luck on your way you
        may go,
      For no forfeit th' opponent imposes.

XXVIII.

27 You lose a stroke when, by a slight mistake,
   A stroke with your opponent's ball you make,
   Unless you get the opponent to agree
   To finish up with yours, and let you be.
   Or you can show the error, without doubt,
   Through his wrong information came about
   (If such mistake's discovered ere he play
   Th' opponent plays a ball from where he lay)
   (N.B. Whenever sides a fair exchange have made
   They keep to such until the hole is played.)

But should it be discovered at the tee
    Before the one or other shall have driven
That one has finished up the recent hole
    With some mistaken ball outside the match,
    'Tis certain then no pardon will be given :
        Th' opponent is free
        To consider that he
        The score may control
        With a merciless soul
And from your score, th' eventful hole will scratch.

XXIX.

39 A penalty stroke never counts to a man
    Though it counts to the score in a manner ;
Rotation of play isn't touched by the ban
    That may alter your chance at the banner.

XXX.

30 By putting green
    We always mean
    (Excepting hazards duly)
    The ground for twenty yards around

Wherein the hole the centre's found
By circumscribing truly.

XXXI.

31   If on the putting green, above defined,
     All loose impediments may be removed,
   But not th' opponent's ball, unless you find
     Within six inches it doth lie, be proved.

XXXII.

33   When the ball is on the putting green
       Before you have played out
     Your side no line or mark can make
       To help you if in doubt.
     Of course your side may point the line,
       But then a touch, though slight,
     By hand or club in doing so
       Will lose the hole outright.

     Anyone of your side may stand the hole
       To mark it whenever you play,
     But all must stand till the stroke is done,
     If moving shield or expose the run ;

For the wind may the line or force control
The hole is the forfeit to pay.

XXXIII.

34 Your caddie or you, with the back of the hand
Lightly brushing, may clear from your way
Sand, snow, or loose earth that is near to the hole
Or is like to intrude on your play.
But of the weighty consequence beware
Of brushing, save across the destined run ;
Or brushing e'en across, if want of care
Admit persuasive pressure, you're undone !
The hole 'twill cost
If rural soil upon the grass impede
Th' intended put, an iron club, at need
Alone permitted, you may then employ
Across the put ; but with no weight destroy
By forfeiting the hole your trembling chance,
For pressure is proclaimed in every circumstance.
Now therefore let us hope the putting line
Except as clearly mentioned you'll decline
To touch with hand or foot or club ; or press
Except before the ball when you address

And then close to the ball your club must be,
For any fault behold the penalty.
    The hole is lost !

XXXIV.

35   Either side is entitled the flag to remove
        When the hole is approached as we've seen ;
    If it's left and you're right it will often improve,
        Though it's red, by a rub of the green.
    If the ball you have played remain touching the
            stave,
        You're entitled the flag to remove ;
    If your ball then roll in the opponent is grave,
        For you're held, and he cannot reprove.

XXXV.

32   When three or more sides are engaged in the play
    Any ball that impedes may be lifted away
    Except on the green to avoid any doubt,
    The further must wait and the nearer hole out.

XXXVI.

7 The first who strikes off from the tee may be said
  What is known as the honour to play ;
  Whoever has won the last hole or a match
  Is the first from the tee to make way !

THE SPECIAL RULES FOR MEDAL PLAY.

I.

3 THE holes should all be changed for Medal-day ;
  And the rule about the greens doth clearly say
    That you'll be disqualified
    If the smallest stroke you've tried
  Ere competing in the round you have to play.

II.

4 Every score shall be kept by a scorer,
    Or each for the other may mark.
  At each hole both the parties shall check it,
    To see that small figures don't lark.

And whenever the round is completed,
　　The score then, the scorer must sign,
And convey to the Sec, or deliver,
　　As he shall his function assign.

III.

10　A competitor shan't play with a professional,
　　　Nor, excepting from his caddie take advice ;
　　But he may employ that person so processional,
　　　The fore caddie—he's a capital device.

IV.

14　All the ordinary rules at this conventicle
　　　Not at variance with those of Medal play
　　Shall apply as though the game were quite iden-
　　　　tical
　　With the matches we engage in every day.

V.

12　The infringement of a rule at once disqualifies ;
　　　A mistake or an intention is the same ;

No allowance is conceded which intensifies
The exactness of a very stringent game.

VI.

The competitor perforce
On the stipulated course,
Who in the fewest strokes shall do the round,
Not evading the conditions
Of the club in competitions
Undoubtedly the winner must be found.

VII.

2   But of course, if two or more
Should return an equal score,
Such ties play off at some convenient hour,
On the same, or any day,
As the Captain shall decide;
Or if he should be away
The competitors abide
By the dictum of the Sec—who has the power.

VIII.

5 Suppose your ball be lost by some ill-luck—
 Unhappy man! you must return and tee
Another ball as near the place 'twas struck
 As may be judged in perfect equity.
For this you lose a stroke.   But if—great joy!—
 Ere you have played, the last ball be descried,
The lost one, being found, you then employ,
 For it remains in play, no loss implied.

IX.

6 When your ball, yourself your clubs or caddie, hits,
 Or if when you play a stroke you hit it twice,
Then you must not lose your temper or your wits,
 But a stroke that swells the scoring in a trice.

X.

7 If your ball should hit an adversary's club,
His caddie or himself it counts a rub;
 And wherever it may lie
 You must play it for the best

Without other penalty,
    Which should keep your mind at rest
But a snob in such a case may try a snub.

XI.

8   You may lift from a hazard of any description ;
    But it counts as two strokes in the scoring sub-
       scription.

XII.

9   All balls shall be holed out, and when the play
    Is on the putting green, the flag away
    Must be removed, and if your ball should lie
    Nearer the hole, you first the hole may try ;
    Or lift your ball, if leaving it might tend,
    Through its position, th' other ball to lend
    Advantage even slight in line or chance,
    Then all the game throughout, whoever thinks
    Another ball if lifted would enhance
    The stroke he plays, may have it off the Links.

XIII.

13   If dispute there should be
      With regard to the play,
      By the Green Committee
      It's determined to-day.

XIV.

11 Though all the clouds should fall like cats and
      dogs,
And Deluge change the putting greens to bogs—
Though Lightning seek to send the subtle flash
With hand so deft to find your keys and cash—
Though Thunder's ample wave your sense be-
      numb—
It boots not what in weather now may come.
Competitors continue still the play,
Or lose their chance upon this gala day.

THE ETIQUETTE OF THE GAME.

"A GOOD LIE."

THE ETIQUETTE OF THE GAME.

ND now, O ye to whom the great in man
Is aught to be revered, peruse the plan
Which must prevail in any game we try,
The sacred outcome of true Charity.

Some men on earth are left who may be found
  To fit a cap upon their neighbour's head ;
But doubtless we upon the golfing ground
  Will fit it well upon our own instead.
For we have many chances to be wise,
Through having much to do with dreadful lies—
With ups and downs, with rubs and lucky hits,
That give the suffering globe plutonic fits—
By puts we do and puts we don't undone,
By where we stopped and where we might have run,
By all th' unhappy things a golfer scorns,

By topping balls when we get out our horns,
By cliques who play as if the green were theirs,
And mashing bounders with discordant airs,
By all the dread vicissitudes of game
That spur the temper, and the mind proclaim
We of all men in holy Wisdom schooled,
By no weak fallacy, should well be fooled.
While on improvement and good manners bent
We shall not say, " Lo ! here the scribbler meant
To have a drive at this or that young man,"
But fit upon ourselves, if that we can,
Correction's cap at every point we name,
To chasten customs in the heroic game.

And now a word of explanation meet,
To save the reckless from their own defeat :
Let him who never having known the ways
Deem not unkind the pointed shafts that graze
His well-intentioned heart, like balls that find
By accident the case that bears the mind.
But let th' instructed guilty rest assured
That quick repentance is the way secured
For comfortable exit from the crime
Of having lost the chance in schooling time

Of training on the all-important plan
That shows the bearing of a gentleman.

And if among your books you find a Locke,
A Bacon, Whateley, and the logic stock ;
Peruse them well before a blatant tongue
Betray you into saying, "this is wrong:"
For it is certain, that right-minded men
Will find him guilty who condemns the pen,
That without malice seeks but to improve
The proper conduct of a game we love.

Some polished ruffians, we do not doubt,
Will close their minds and rudely chuck us out
For this prepared we shall not seek to chide,
But feel requited by the salient fact
That if our pen have pierced the yielding hide,
They'll never more forget when in the act
Of some translucent folly, which will tend
To spoil a stroke, and force them, in the end,
Through very selfishness and shame to yield
To some good manners in the golfing field.

When at the tee, we wait till those before
Have played their second and are out of range,
The ignorant discard the range with "fore!"
And play, regardless of a risk so strange.

The man who knowing plays the game like this
Betrays a nature that is much amiss;
Reproach him not! His genius may trapan
The ways and customs of a gentleman!

If with the course well cleared in front we find
Our foozledom is keeping all behind,
We let good players pass—or lift and go
To where the green is clear or play is slow;
The man who stands on what he calls his rights
And keeps all back behind is quite unfit
To have his name upon the roll of knights
Who, knowing courtesy, should act on it.
That man is he who often may be seen,
While others wait, to try again the green.
That man who when he plays a single ball
Will neither move nor listen to the call;
'Tis true he may be said to stand the fire,
But that won't yield the temper we desire,

Although it softens steel it hardens men
And points the satire of a nimble pen.

Again, and yet how evident methinks
The man is found on every golfing links
Himself availing of the right to drive
Ahead of those before, when on the course,
Who hits away to keep the game alive
And calls his " fore " with insufficient force ;
Some day such foolish people may expect
A striking incident to tell direct
Th' astounding silliness of habits rude
That sin the soul of noble brotherhood.

When calling " fore," be sure the party hears
And sees before you play, or grief may come !
Some strike the ball, and then observe it nears
The placid victim ere they shout—then home
The ball goes whizzing, gets him in the eye,
And so the man before begins to cry;
Of course the man in front, if wanting strokes,
And by his play the man behind provokes,
Yet give him some small chance lest he prefer
To get behind the strokes, that do not err.

M

The man in front well hit behind before
Will often when in front expect some more,
And thus when every stalwart mother's son
Shall have been hit before and left behind
True wisdom will be taxed to see the fun
Of such queer tricks of mortal hand and mind.
The party first upon the measured green
Should not be hampered by the fear of death
From wild approaches far too often seen
Played by those men who cannot hold the breath
Of flippant gibe which—just to put it mild—
Would do small credit to a wayward child.
The man who plays like this you may depend
Has many faults of character to mend,
Like him who on the putting green essays—
When forward's clear—and all behind delays.

"When on the stroke" the Etiquette reproves
That man who goes in front or even moves.

Who is not still upon the stroke may find
Suspicion roused that is not always kind.
Some men may class him with the paltry fool
Who pays his life before he's in at Pool

So that by making that which should be sure,
A doubtful thing, his life he may secure.

Again we should remember at the tee
In starting for a hole when playing golf
Your ball upon the ground should never be—
If you play last—until the opponent's off.

Then if your ball be lost you clear the way
For those behind to pass you in the play—
Three balls must yield to every passing two
And two who don't to two who play the round ;
When playing single, all shall pass—for you
Have not a raison-d'être upon the ground.

As the green is not meant to be carted away,
You'll remember those divots you cut when you play
Should be nicely replaced by your caddie or you
With the roots to the earth and the blades to the dew.

N.B. The reckoning of the strokes is kept by the
terms " the odd " " two more " " three more," etc. and
" one off three " " one off two " the like. The reckoning
of the holes is kept by the terms so many " holes up "
or " all even " and so many " to play."

INDEX TO ST. ANDREW'S RULES.

The Italics refer to Rules for Medal Play.

GLOSSARY OF TERMS NOT EXPLAINED IN THE RULES AND ETIQUETTE.

Approach. A stroke that may reach the hole.

Baff. To strike the ground and the ball simultaneously with a wooden club.

Be up. Be as far as the hole.

Bolt. The hole is bolted when the ball goes in with unusual speed.

Carry. The distance the ball goes before coming to ground.

Cut. Under-cut is a back spin on a ball. Slice-cut is diagonal right and back spin.

Dead. When the ball is so near the hole as to be certain of going in on the next stroke it is "Dead."

Draw. A divided match is a "draw." A ball drawn off the line to the left is also called a "draw." It comes off the heel of a Bulger or the toe of an old-fashioned hollow faced club, or off any club badly swung.

Green. "Play through the green" is used for playing along the grass anywhere. "On the Green" means on the putting green.

Heel. To heel a ball off the old-fashioned club meant to strike it with the heel of the club or that part of the face nearest the handle.

Hole open. Means that no obstacle lies between your ball and the hole: one may play for such a position " To open up the hole."

Hole high. A ball is said to be "hole high" when a stroke has driven as far as the hole (in the direction of the said hole as a matter of course).

Hole out. To play all strokes necessary to get the ball actually into the hole.

Keen. An expression in curling and golf. When the ice is very smooth, and the stone slides easily, the ice is " keen." When the green is smooth and hard and the ball runs easily, the ground is " keen."

Lie. The place where the ball lies. The ball lies in a lie.

Loft. To send the ball a-loft. " A lofter," a stroke that goes aloft. Also used for the ground where a ball falls as "a running loft" where sloping ground makes the ball run.

Press. To press is to put unnecessary force into a stroke.

Run. The travel of a ball on the ground. " Run up," to approach the hole with a putter or in any way along the ground.

Short. Playing short is knocking the ball so that it does not reach the hole : or in a long stroke, keeping back intentionally.

Slice. Play across the line of required direction always sends a well struck ball to the right of the spot it is aimed for.

Stimie. When one ball gets in the way of another in the line of the hole it produces a stimie. We hear a man say he is stimied by a tree. This is not inappropriate if the word be derived from the Broad Scotch of " Stay me."

Tee. A minute pyramid of sand on which to place the ball at the first stroke in each hole. (Don't take much of it!)

Toe. That part of the club farthest from the handle : " to toe," to play off the toe.

Turn. " The turn," when half the match is played the players are said to be " at the turn."

A GOLFING EPISODE.

A GOLFING EPISODE.

A, *B*, play *C*, *D*, for considerable stakes. Their caddies look like the ordinary simple Sandy but they are a fly clique.

Fly No. 1 carries for *A*, No. 2 for *C*, No. 3 for *B*, and No. 4 for *D*. Their Christian names (if they are in any way Christians,) are No. 1, Baldy—No. 2, Jock —No. 3, Airchie—No. 4, Jemmie.

SCENE I.

Enter Fly No. 1, *in confidential conversation with* Fly No. 2.

No. 1.

 ' SAYIN' Jock! ma maun's a fair clipper. He's promised me a sovereign if he wuns this mautch. Div ye no think ye could gie's a haun i' the gheme, man?

No. 2. Hoo's thaht tae be dune, think ye?

No. 1. Gin ye'll maunage the mater A'll staun ye five bob for yersel. A bit stramp in a gressy lie here and there—an airn instead o' a cleek—or the like, 'll dae the job for you an me. An' ye cannae maunage that gate, syne there's aye the chaunce o' a lost baa'.

No. 2. Din wi' you, Baldy. A'll dae the trick.

SCENE II.

(*Enter* Flies, Nos. 3 and 4.)

No. 4. Maun Airchie, there's a lot o' siller gaun on this mautch the day.

No. 3. Aye! they big folk can play for a pound whaure we maun be content wi' the pennies : buit d'ye ken the Captain's promised Baldy Scott a sovereign if the mautch gangs their gait. D'ye no think ye could get a bigger bid frae the Major an' syne keep yer een aboot ye?

No. 4. Weel, an that could be brocht aboot, what wud ye propose, Airchie?

No. 3. What wud A propose?—A wud jest propose that gin ye'll divide the money wi' me A'll show ye hoo tae wun as share 's death.

No. 4. Aweel! aweel Airchie, A'm on wi' you, for the Major's promised me a fiver gin oo wun the mautch, and A'm no sic a fuil as tae think oor side's gunn'ae wun 'ithout some luck in oor favour.—Buit what's yer thocht aboot it?

No. 3. (*sotto voce.*) Well, i' the first place keep yer ee on yer mate an see that your men dinnae play yin

o' the happin cavies [1] for A selt twa o' thum tae Jock
for half-a-croon, the day afore yesterday. 'I the next
place, dinnae lose sicht o' yer baa. It micht be lost
whiles. Keep close tae Jock : an' keep yer wits aboot
ye, a guide lie whiles maks a braw stroke ! leave the
rest tae me.

SCENE III.

No. 4. (*Aside to* Major D.) I wud like ye tae wun
this mautch Sir—There's a guid breeze on the day, an'
A've gottten twa three special sizes. Gin ye'll persuade
Mr. C. to play them a' the round, an' dinnae mack ony
remark aboot it, but jist tak them, they're markit wi' my
ain mark an maybe ye'll gie me a bit screed to say what
ye think o' them, an it'll help the sellin o' ithers. Yae
size is heavy an' haurd on the clubs buit it'll tell again
the wund. The ither size is sma', buit a devil to gang
wi' the wund. (*The* Major *takes the balls and arranges
with* C. *to carry out* Jemmie's *proposal*). (No. 4. *goes
over to his mate* No. 2.)

No. 4. (*Sotto voce.*) Has C promised ye onything
gin oo hae success, Jock ?

No. 2. No a make !

No. 4. They're no like the ither side ! A'm

[1] A kind of hopping game: the name here applies to a ball
made up with a slight load of metal, so that it runs with enough
bias to spoil a put.

thinkin', man, oo micht maunage to gar oor side loss an' syne Baldy wad hae to staun the drinks. He'll hae a sovereign !

No. 2. A'm on wi' ye for that ghem ; an' A can help ye tae gin ye like !

No. 4. Hoo that, Jock ?

No. 2. A've gotten twa happin cavies i' ma pooch !

No. 4. Happin cavies ! What's that, man ?

No. 2. Jest bonny baas wi' a wee bit airn i' the gutty to pit them off the line.

No. 4. Let's hae a look at them ; man Jock, oo'll dae the trick ! (*The unsuspecting* No. 2 *hands the foul balls to* No. 4.)

No. 4. Weel, Jock, ye've gotten yer wits aboot ye. That's a clever invention. A'll find the richt place for pittin' down they bonny things for ye.

(The players are well matched. At the turn the game is all even. At the tenth hole, however, B's ball does not make way so well, and on the putting green loses the hole by a slight bias. The knowing *No.* 3. remarks that Mr. B. " jist drew in his airm a wee bit." *No.* 2 now asks *No.* 4 to give him one of the happin cavies, but *No.* 4 persuades him that there is lots of time.

Three more holes are divided. One up to C D, and five to play. *No.* 2 becomes anxious and gets well forward, probably with a view to bringing pressure to bear upon the next stroke by squeezing the ball into the sod. *No.* 4 lets him take his way, but keeps a steady eye upon him. *No.* 2 achieves his purpose, but *No.* 4 coming up with Major D., who plays next, succeeds in the most subtle manner in putting the ball right, while he is drawing the Major's attention to the line and distance. To lull suspicion he recommends the driving iron instead of the brassie, and *No.* 2 is disagreeably surprised at the ball getting away as well as usual. Mr. B. has driven out of the line, and got into the bent. *No.* 3, with apparent anxiety, hurries forward to find the ball. He finds one of the genus happin cavie, but in a horrid lie, while mysteriously the proper ball climbs into his pocket. Airchie assumes intense disgust at the bad luck, as he calls it. Three strokes to get out finishes A and B's chance of that hole without bias in putting. Two up and four to play, and all attributed to a bad put and a bad piece of luck. The unsuspecting victims go on philosophically with the game.

No. 4 hands back to *No.* 2 the foul balls, telling him it is no use trying them, as the Major specially orders that they keep on with the same two balls).

No. 2. A'll look oot for a lost baa then, Jemmie.

No. 4. Ye neednae faush! A've chineged my mind. It's no jist honest tae tak' a man's mony for caryin' an' thaen tae daumage his chance. Gin oo dinnae get onything tae oorsels, oo'll aye can expeck oor reward accordin' to the Bible for suffering for righteous-

N

ness' sake. (*No.* 2 doesn't see that. He attempts a lost ball and manages it.)

No. 4. Ye've thrown the baa ower the whuns ; here's another like it. Ye've cheated your side. Pit that down an cheat the ithers tae, or A'll explain matters to the Major an' hae yer bonny happin cavies turned oot when yer pooches is ripet. Ye're a dishonest deil, man !

(*No.* 2 is sold : no escape from his righteous comrade. He drops the ball in advance of the search party, and has to shout with apparent gladness that the ball is found. The match went the way of the most money, and only two men knew the reason why.)

3   4 2

AFTER THE MATCH.

HANDICAP CHART.

HOLES AT WHICH STROKE ALLOWANCES ARE TO BE TAKEN.

1	10																	
2	7	13																
3	7	10	13															
4	4	8	12	16														
5	4	8	10	12	16													
6	3	6	9	12	15	18												
7	3	6	9	10	12	15	18											
8	2	4	6	8	12	14	16	18										
9	2	4	6	8	10	12	14	16	18									
10	2	4	6	7	8	12	13	14	16	18								
11	2	4	5	7	8	10	11	13	14	16	17							
12	2	3	5	6	7	9	11	13	14	15	17	18						
13	2	3	5	6	7	9	10	11	13	14	15	17	18					
14	3	4	5	6	7	8	9	11	12	13	14	15	16	17				
15	3	4	5	6	7	8	9	10	11	12	13	14	15	16	17			
16	2	3	4	5	6	7	8	9	10	11	12	13	14	15	16	17		
17	2	3	4	5	6	7	8	9	10	11	12	13	14	15	16	17	18	
18	1	2	3	4	5	6	7	8	9	10	11	12	13	14	15	16	17	18

MATCH-PLAY ODDS.

In singles.—¾ of difference between handicap allowances.

In foursomes.—⅜ of difference between the aggregate handicap allowances on either side.

A ½ stroke, or over, shall count as 1.   Smaller fractions count as 0.

SEE TABLE BELOW :—

Handicap difference	STROKE ALLOWANCES		Handicap difference	STROKE ALLOWANCES	
	Singles	Foursomes		Singles	Foursomes
1	1	0	19	14	7
2	2	1	20	15	8
3	2	1	21	16	8
4	3	2	22	17	8
5	4	2	23	17	9
6	5	2	24	18	9
7	5	3	25	19	9
8	6	3	26	20	10
9	7	3	27	20	10
10	8	4	28	21	11
11	8	4	29	22	11
12	9	5	30	23	11
13	10	5	31	23	12
14	11	5	32	24	12
15	11	6	33	25	12
16	12	6	34	26	13
17	13	6	35	26	13
18	14	7	36	27	14

INDEX.

CHISWICK PRESS :—CHARLES WHITTINGHAM AND CO.
TOOKS COURT, CHANCERY LANE, LONDON.

SD - #0035 - 280423 - C0 - 229/152/11 - PB - 9780259488729 - Gloss Lamination